MEDIEVAL
Coloring Book

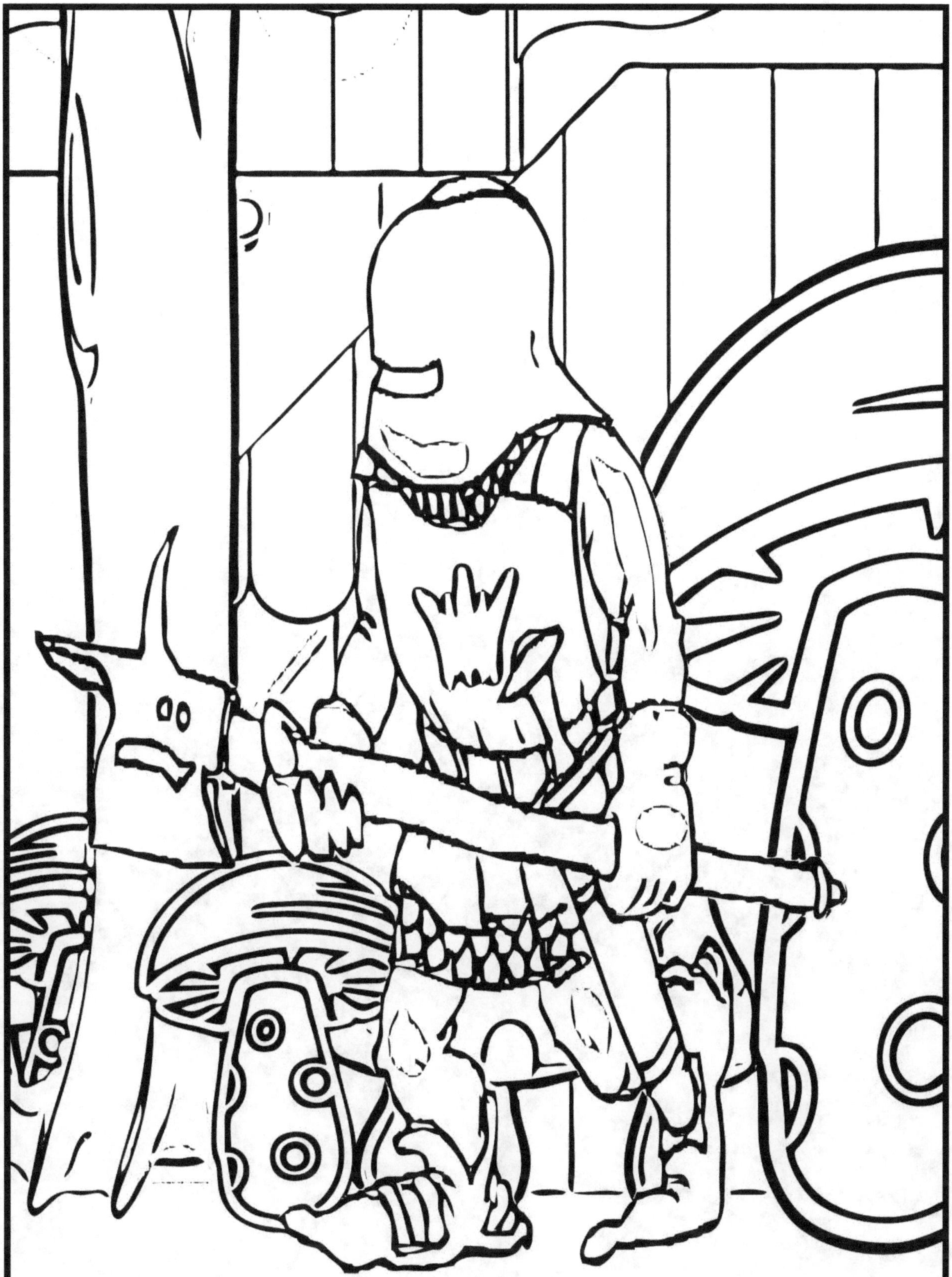

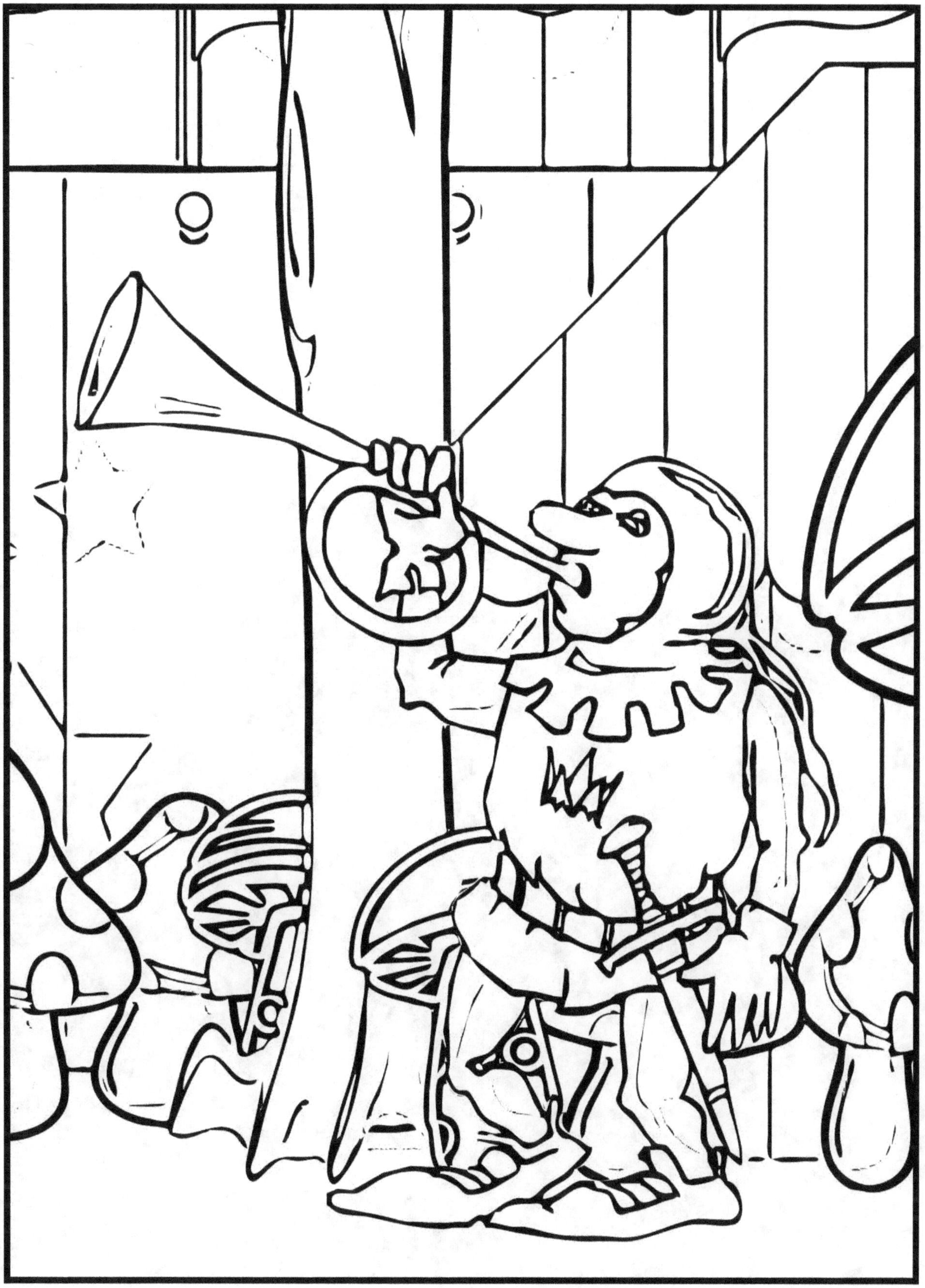

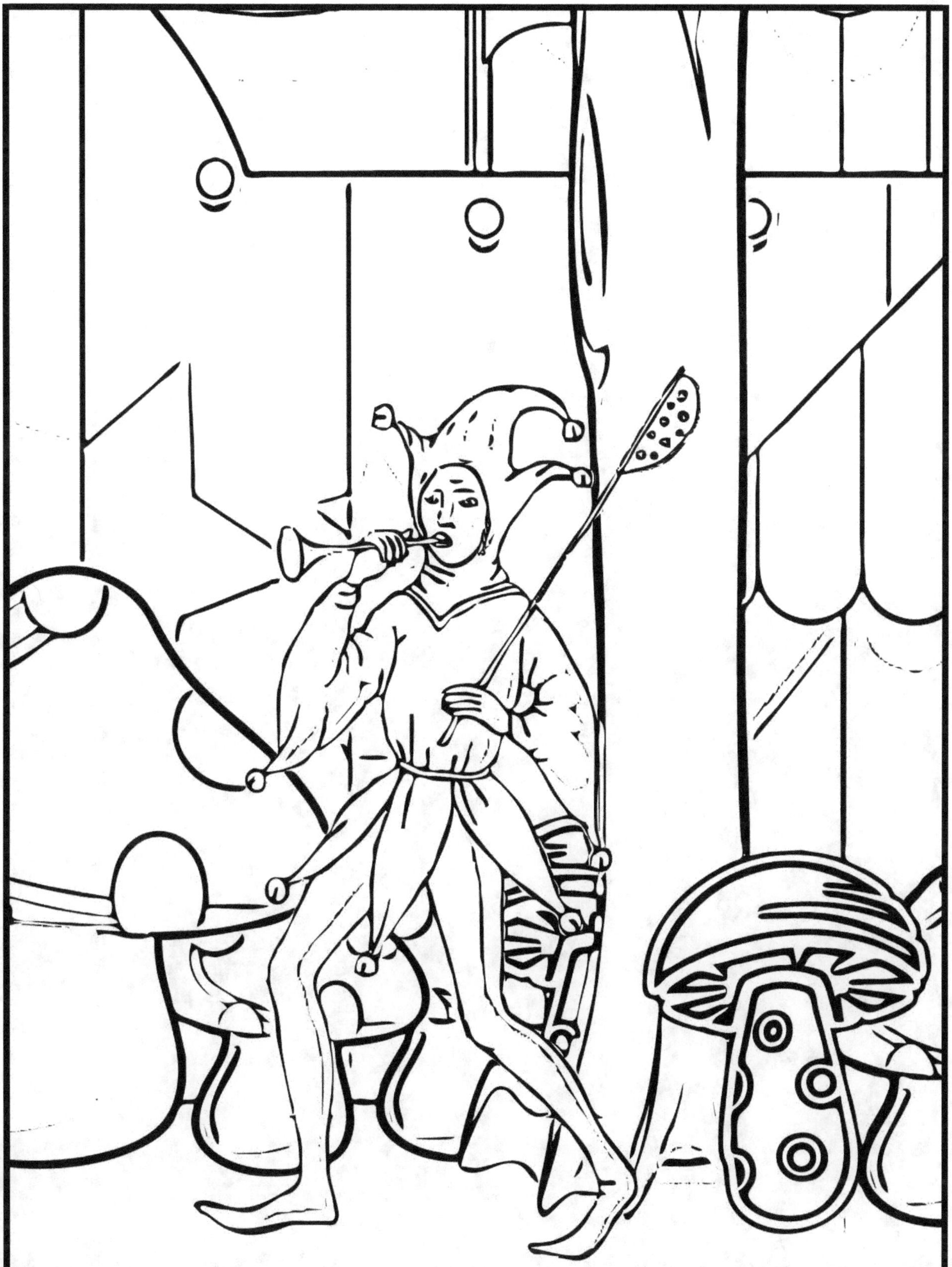

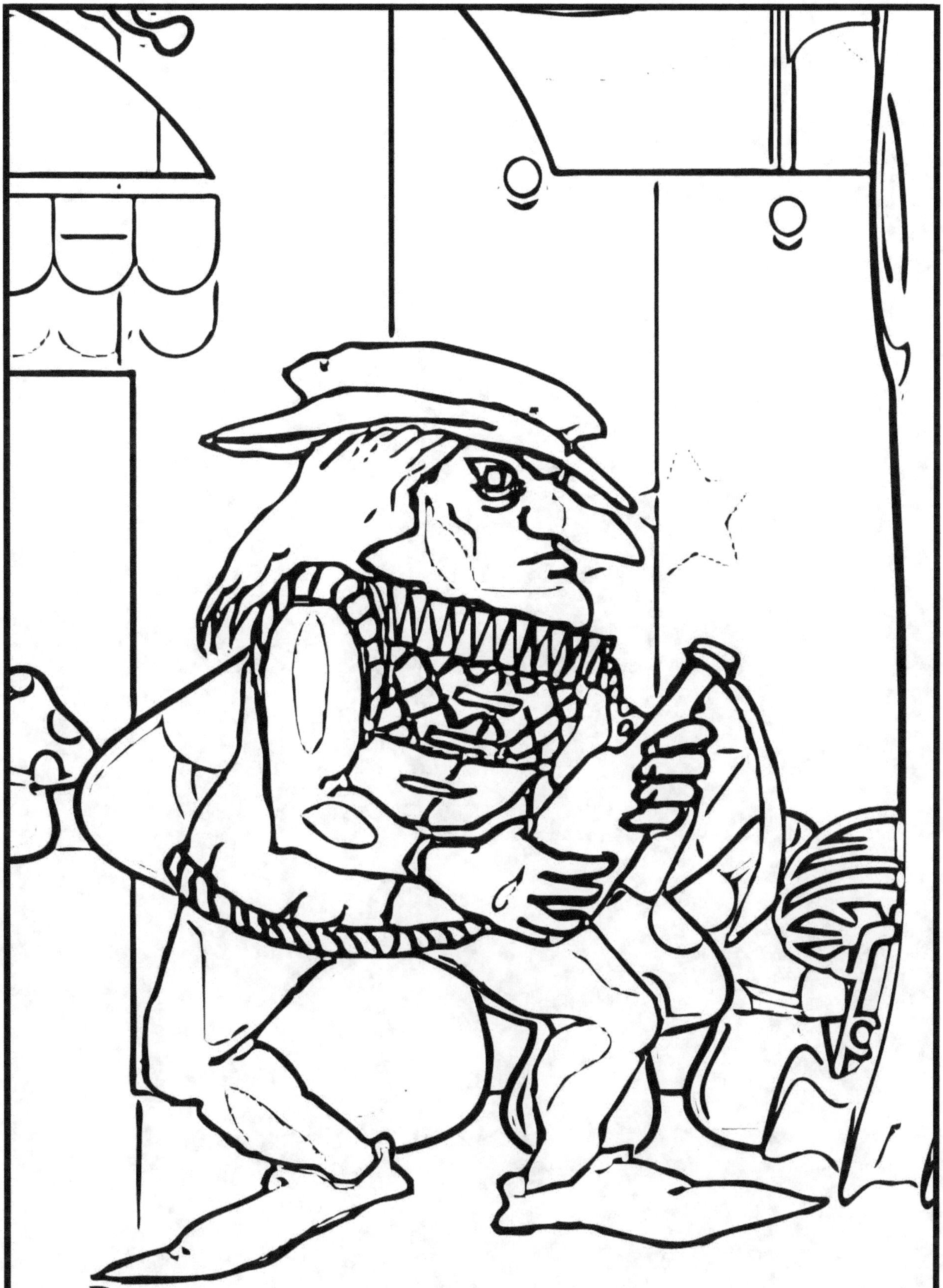

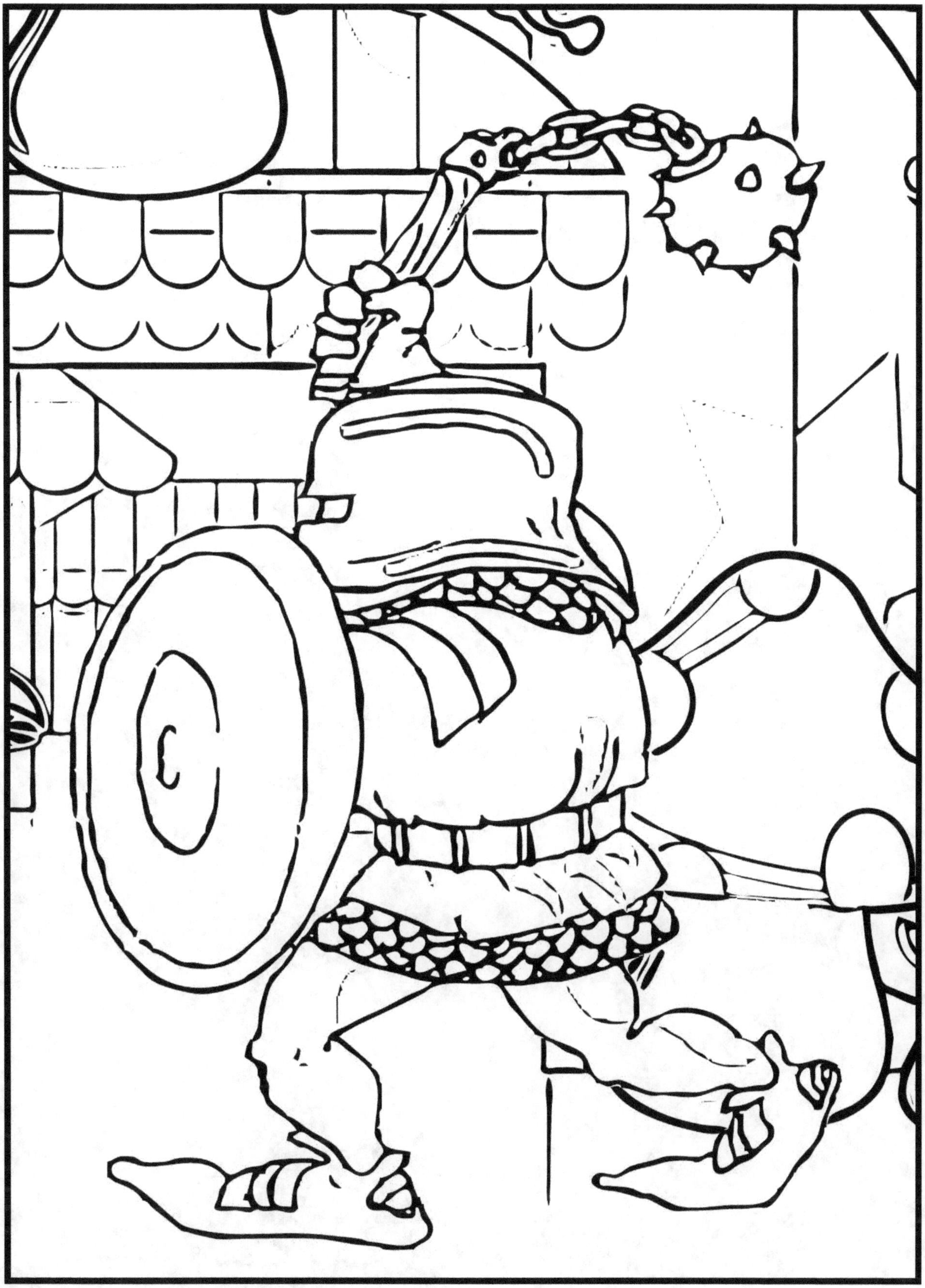

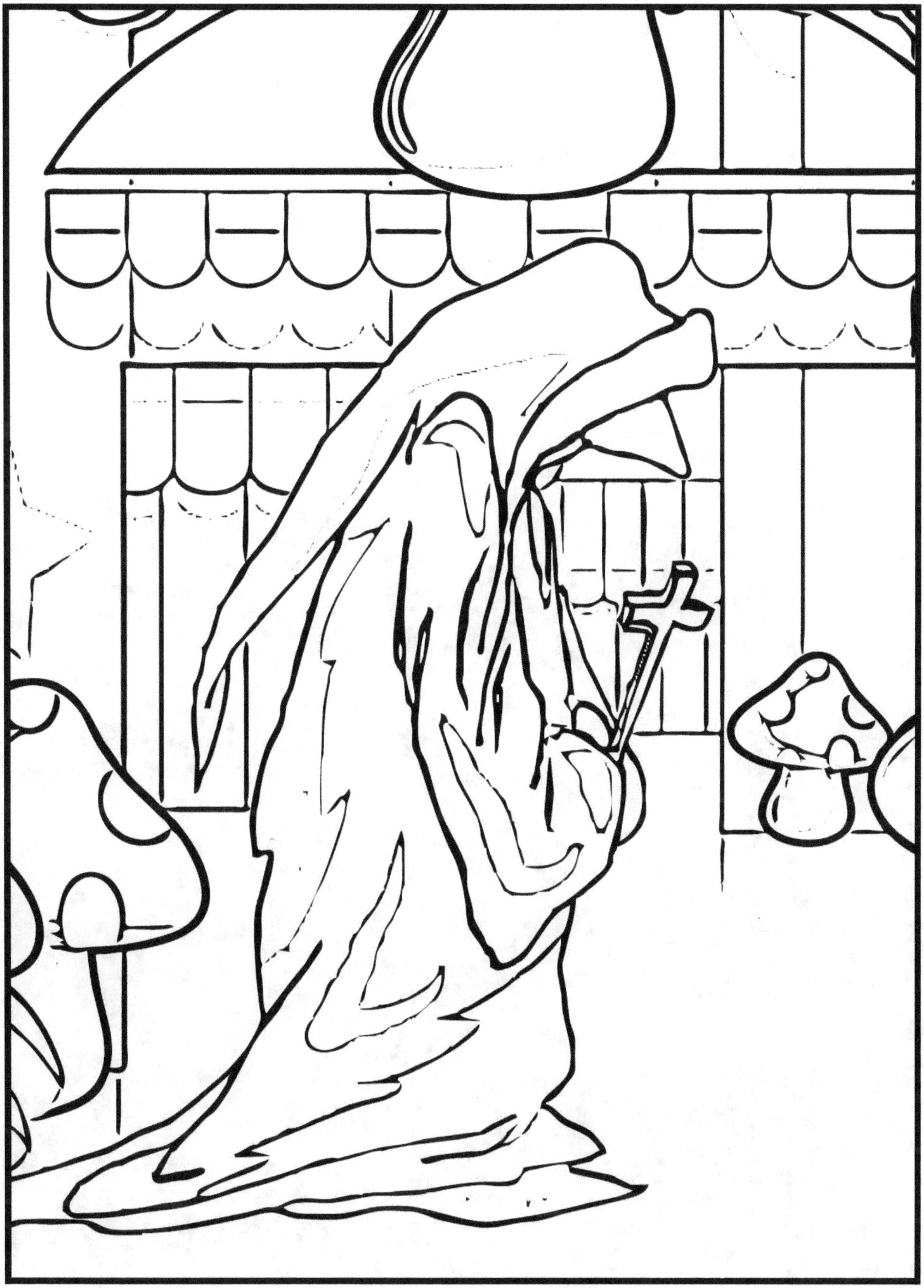

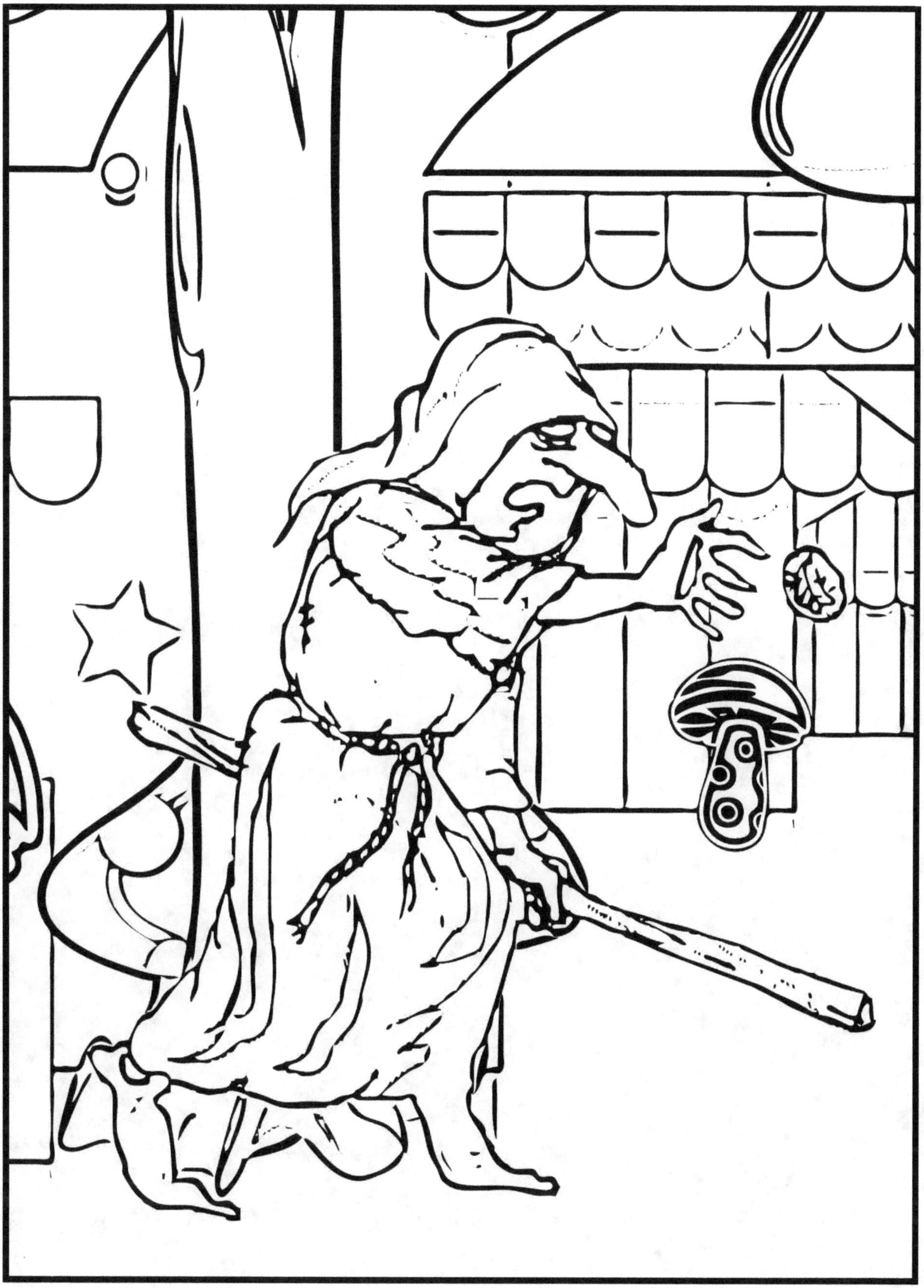

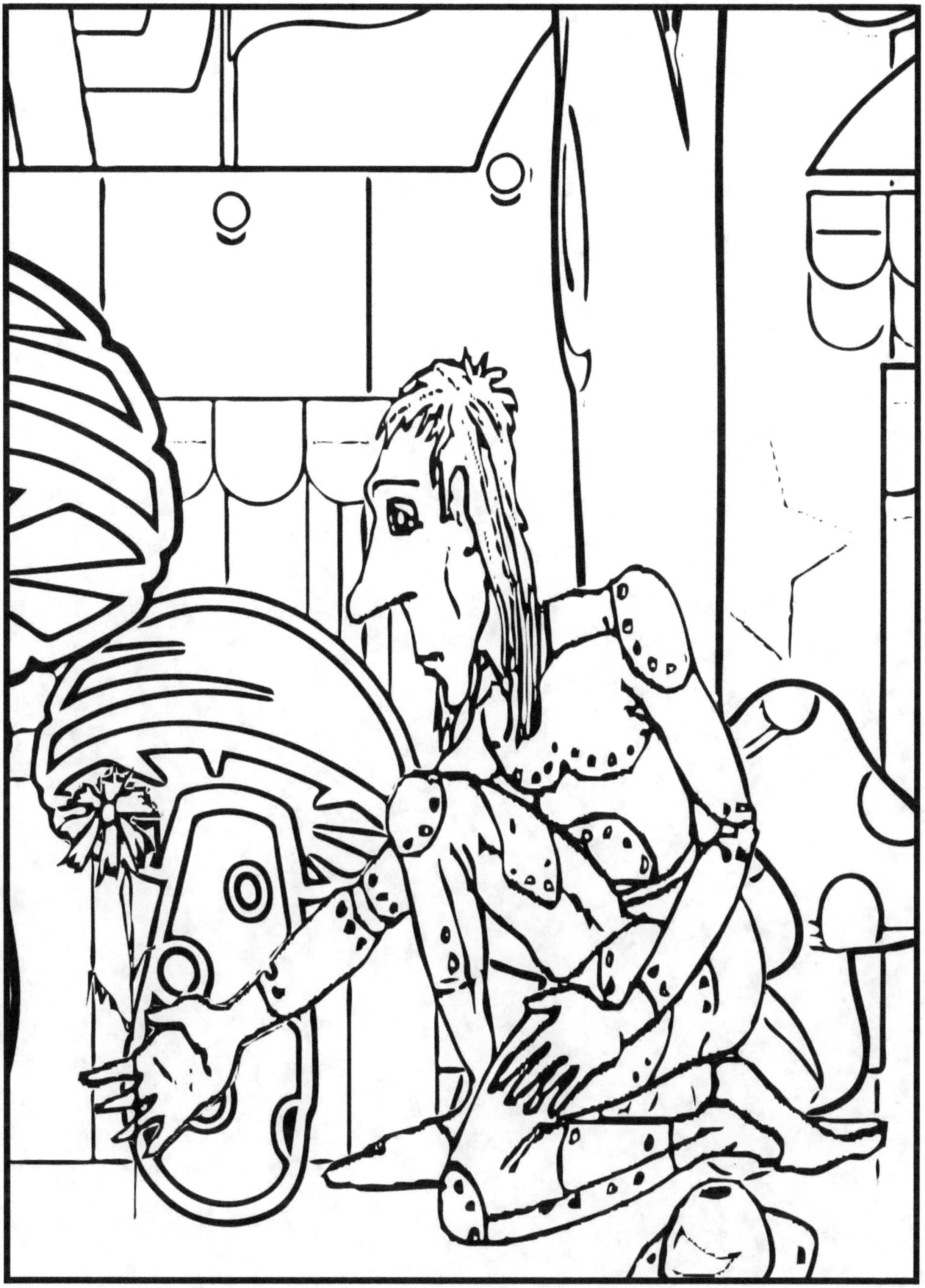

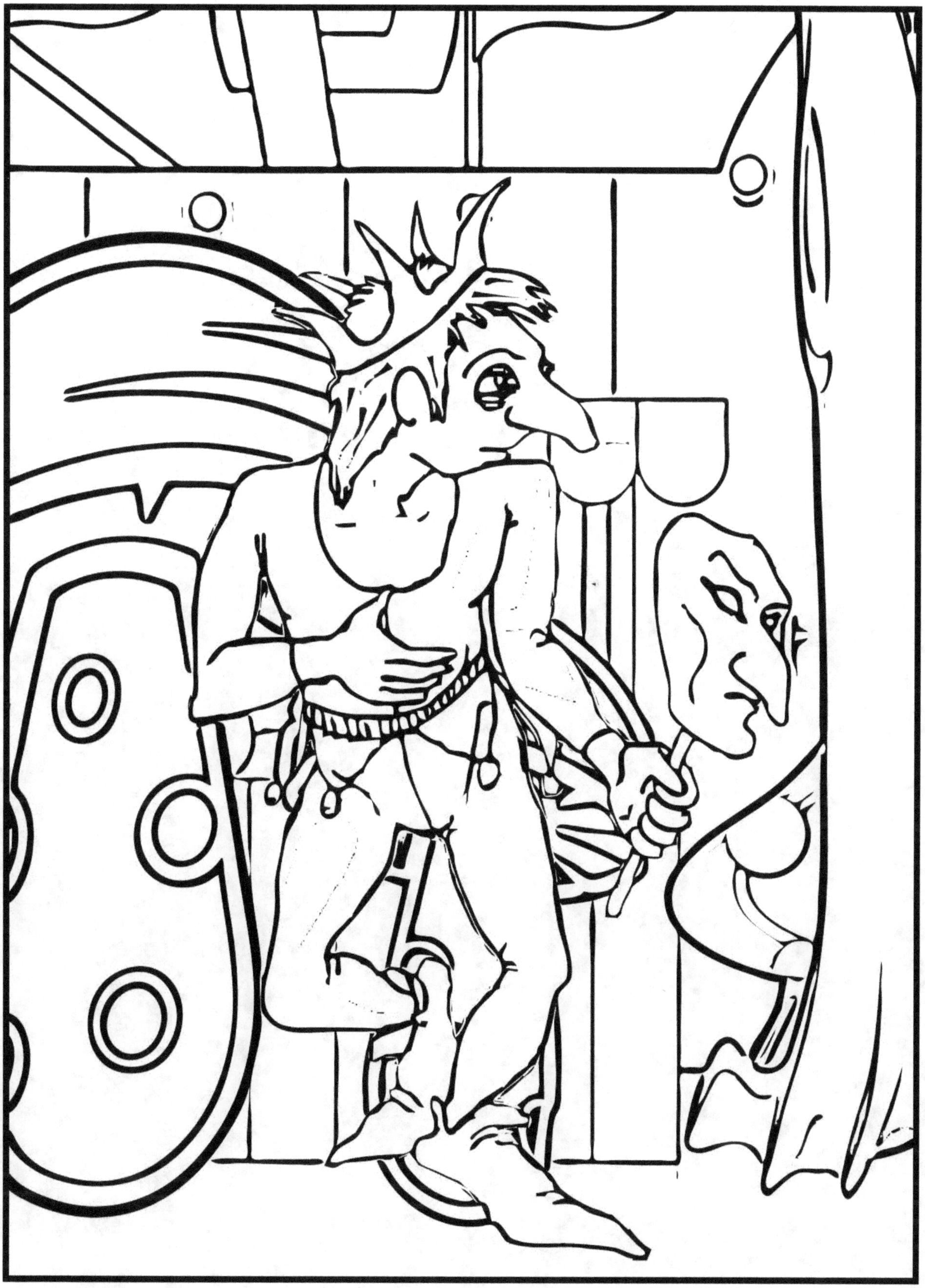

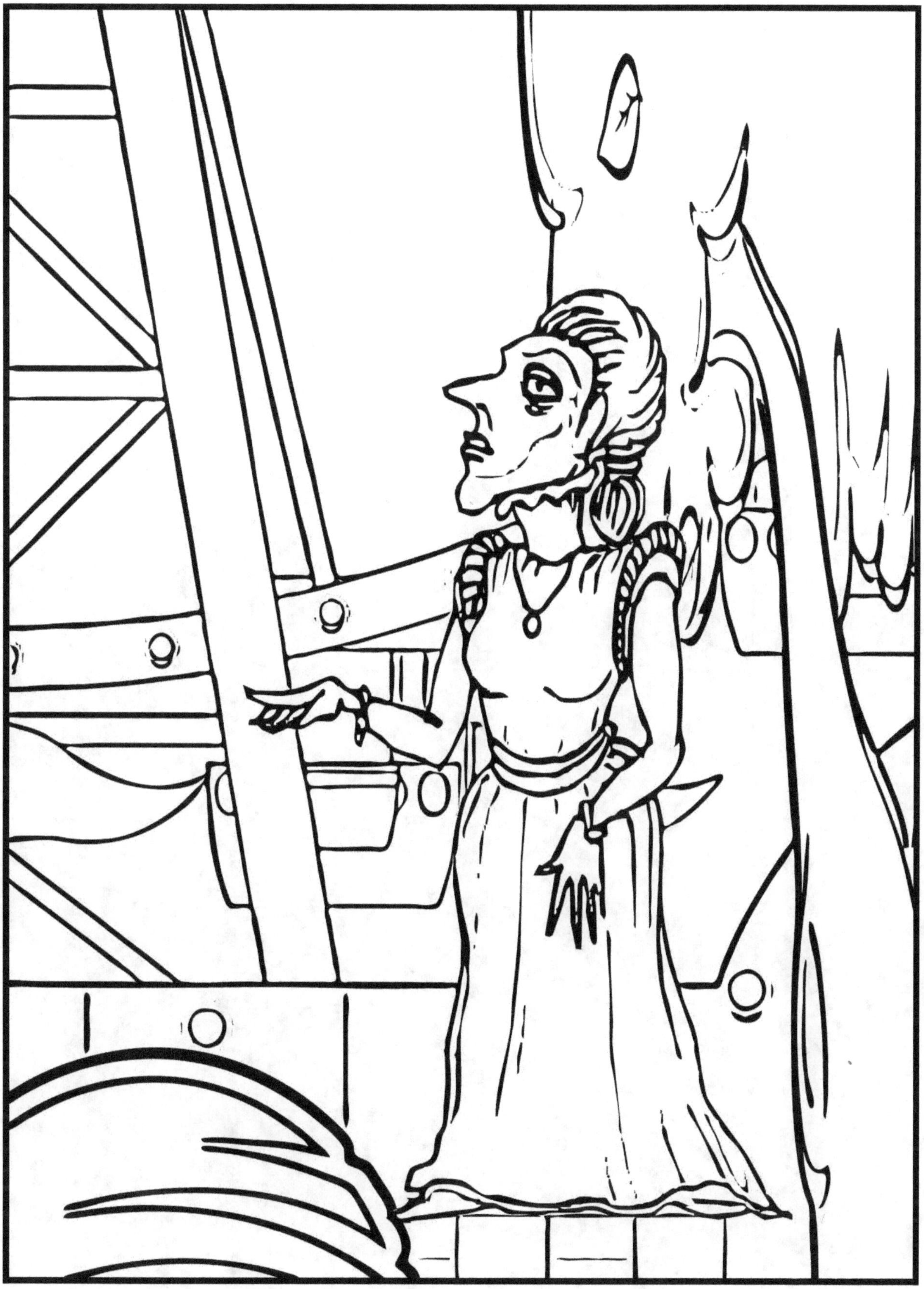

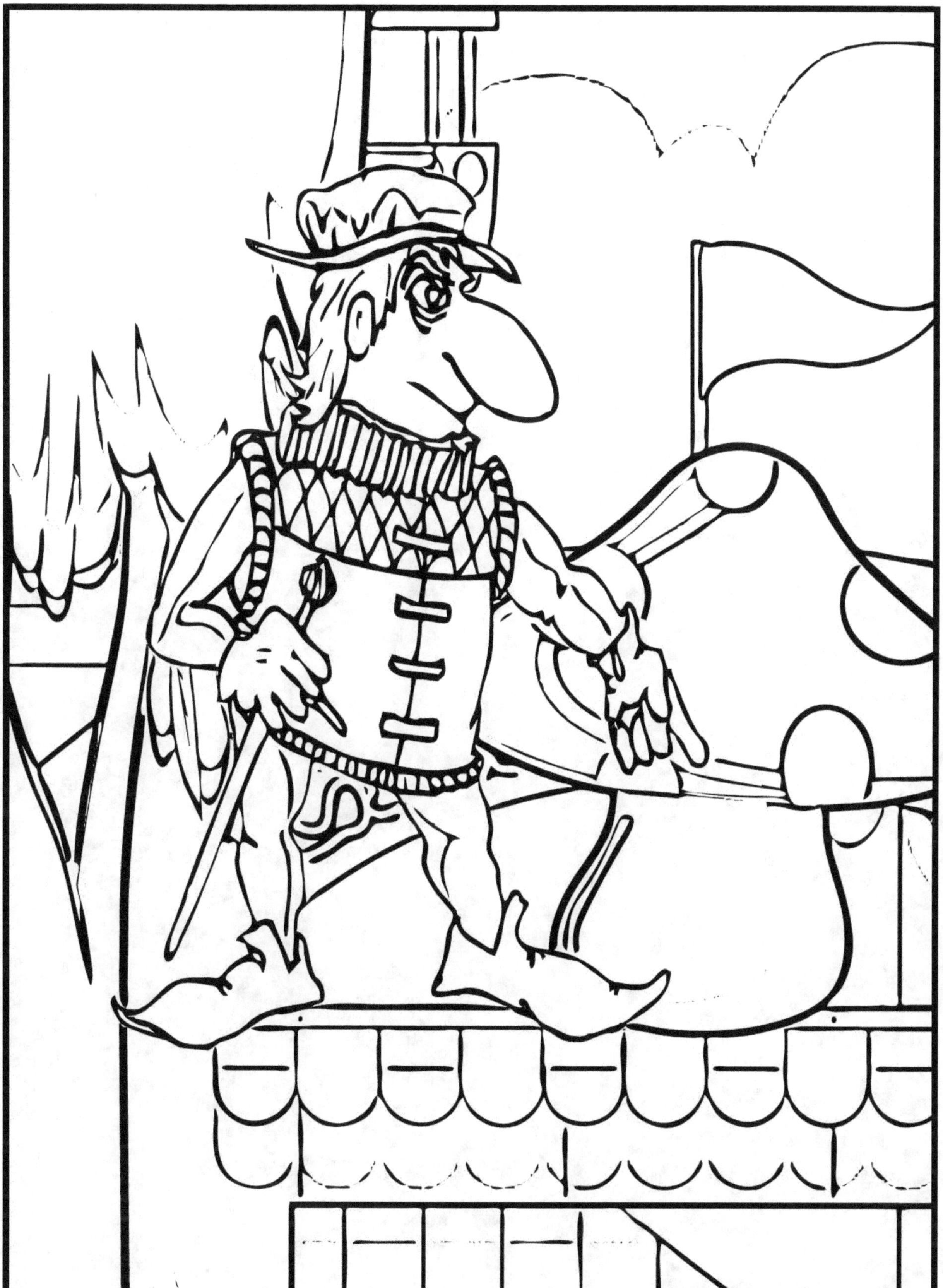

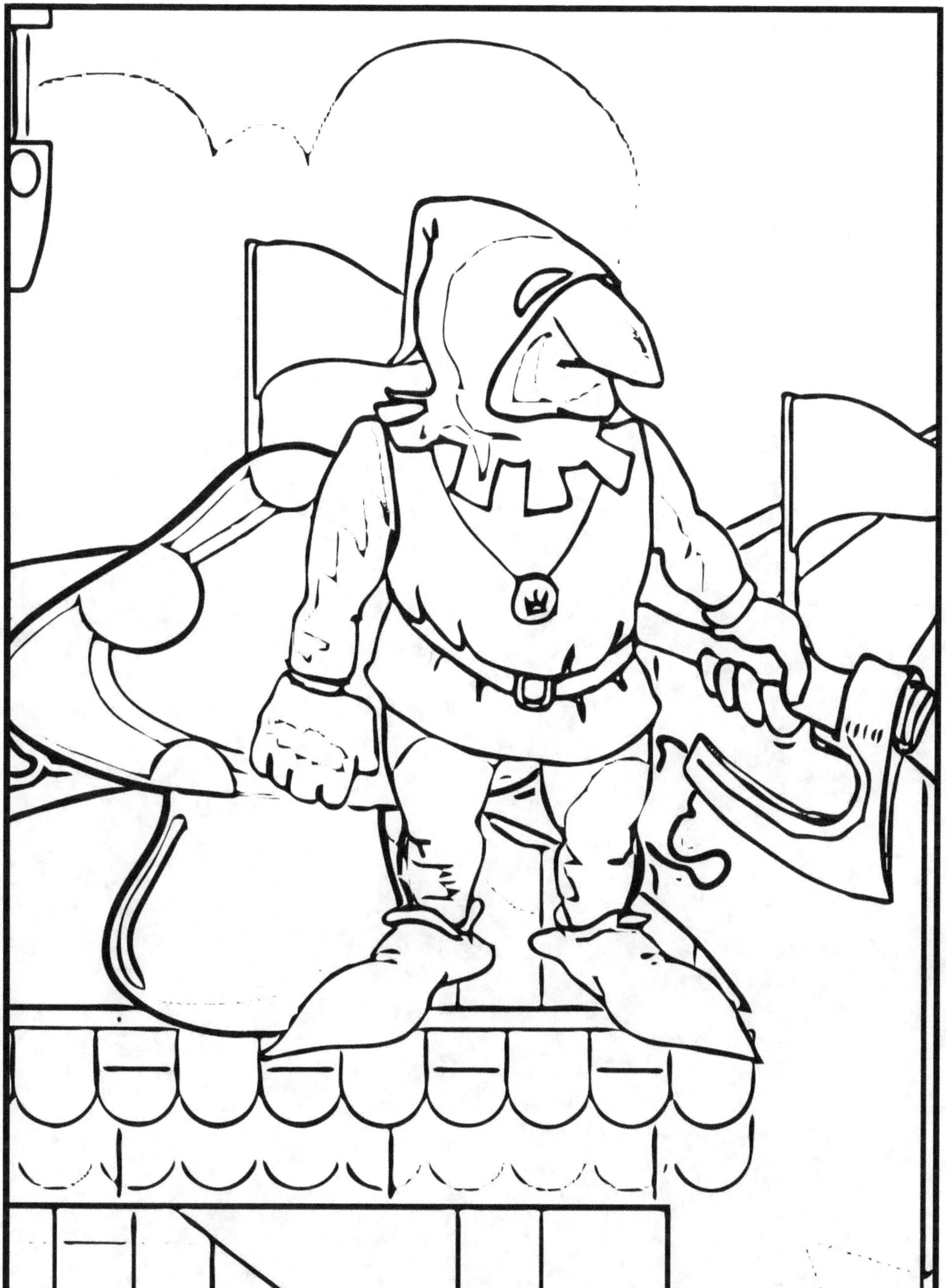

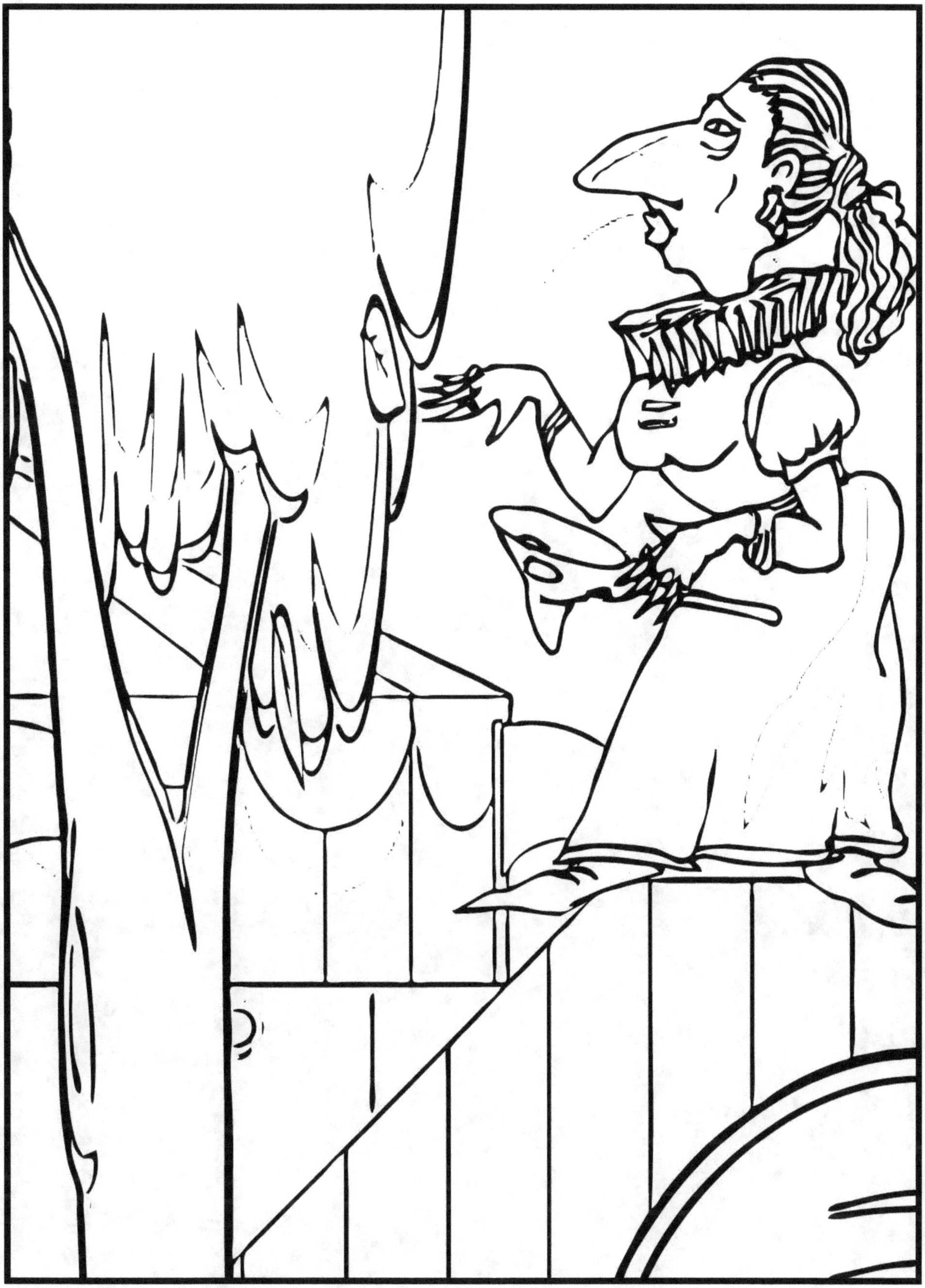

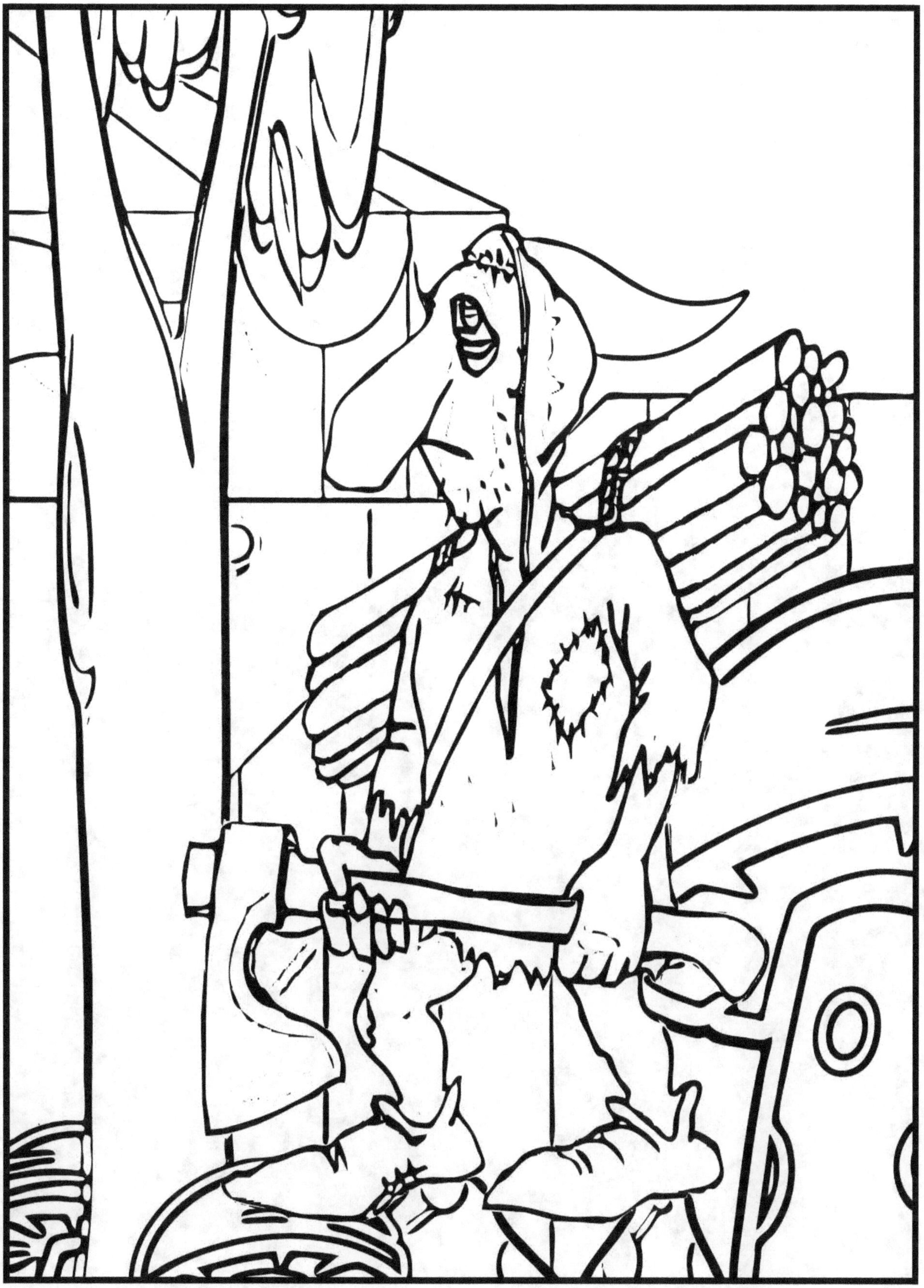

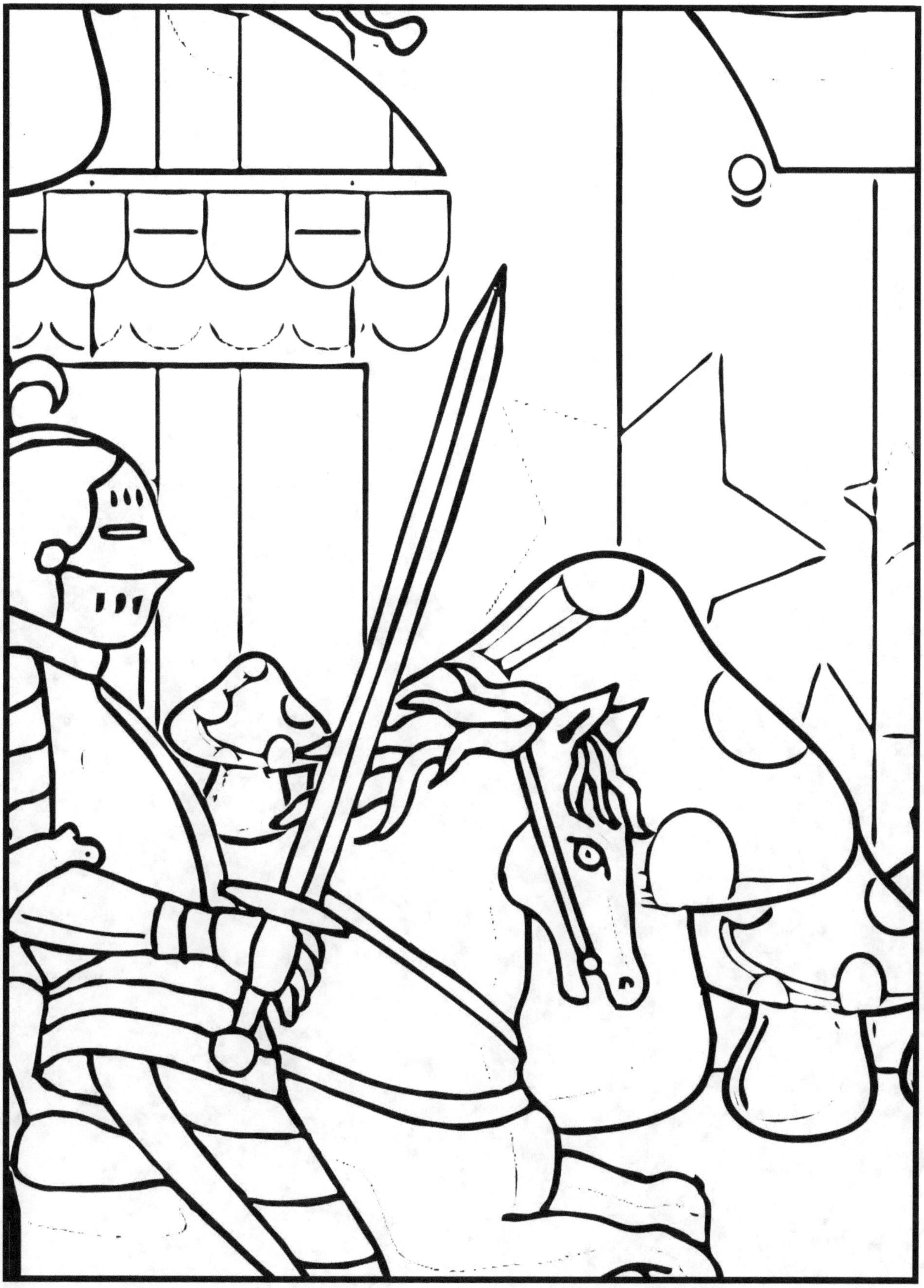

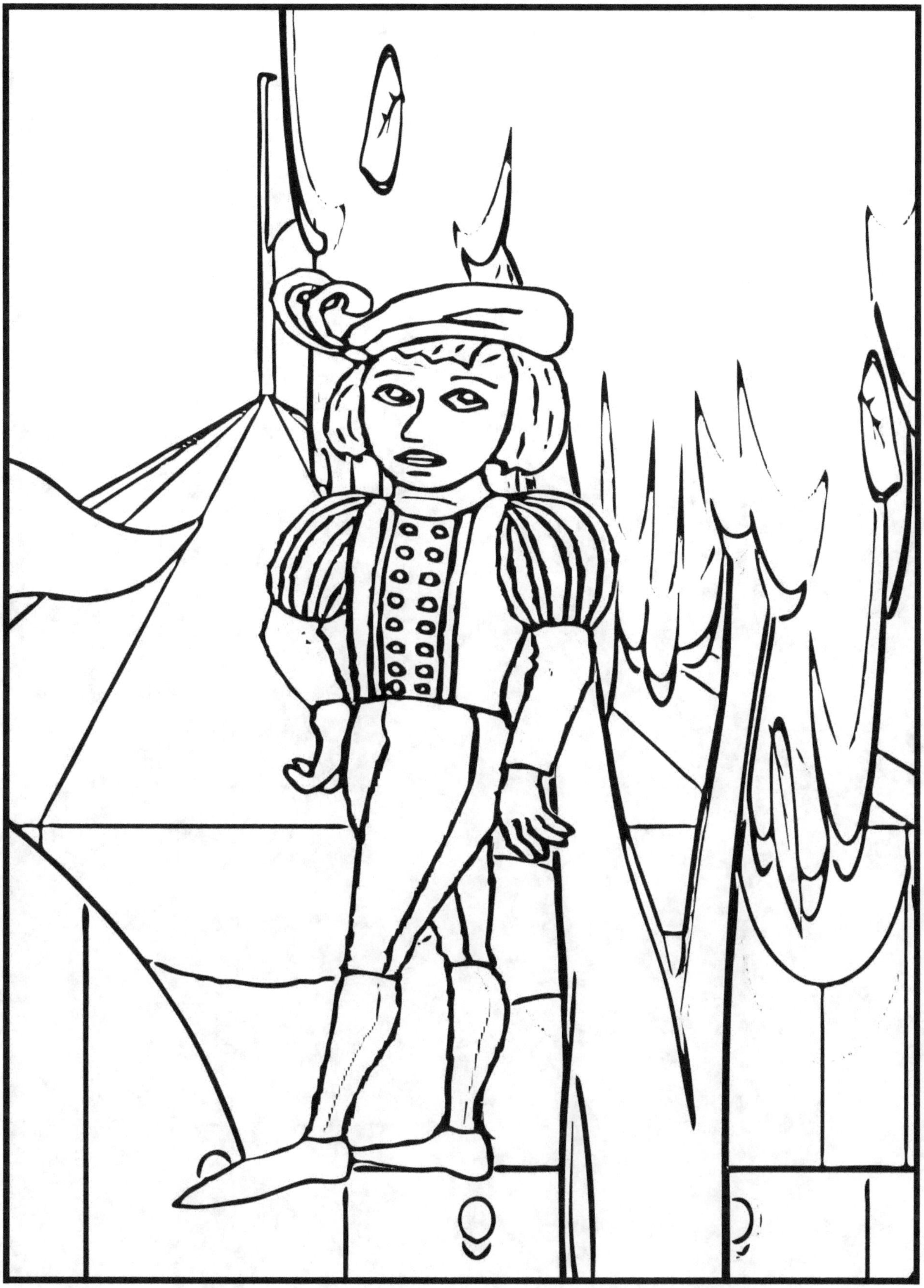

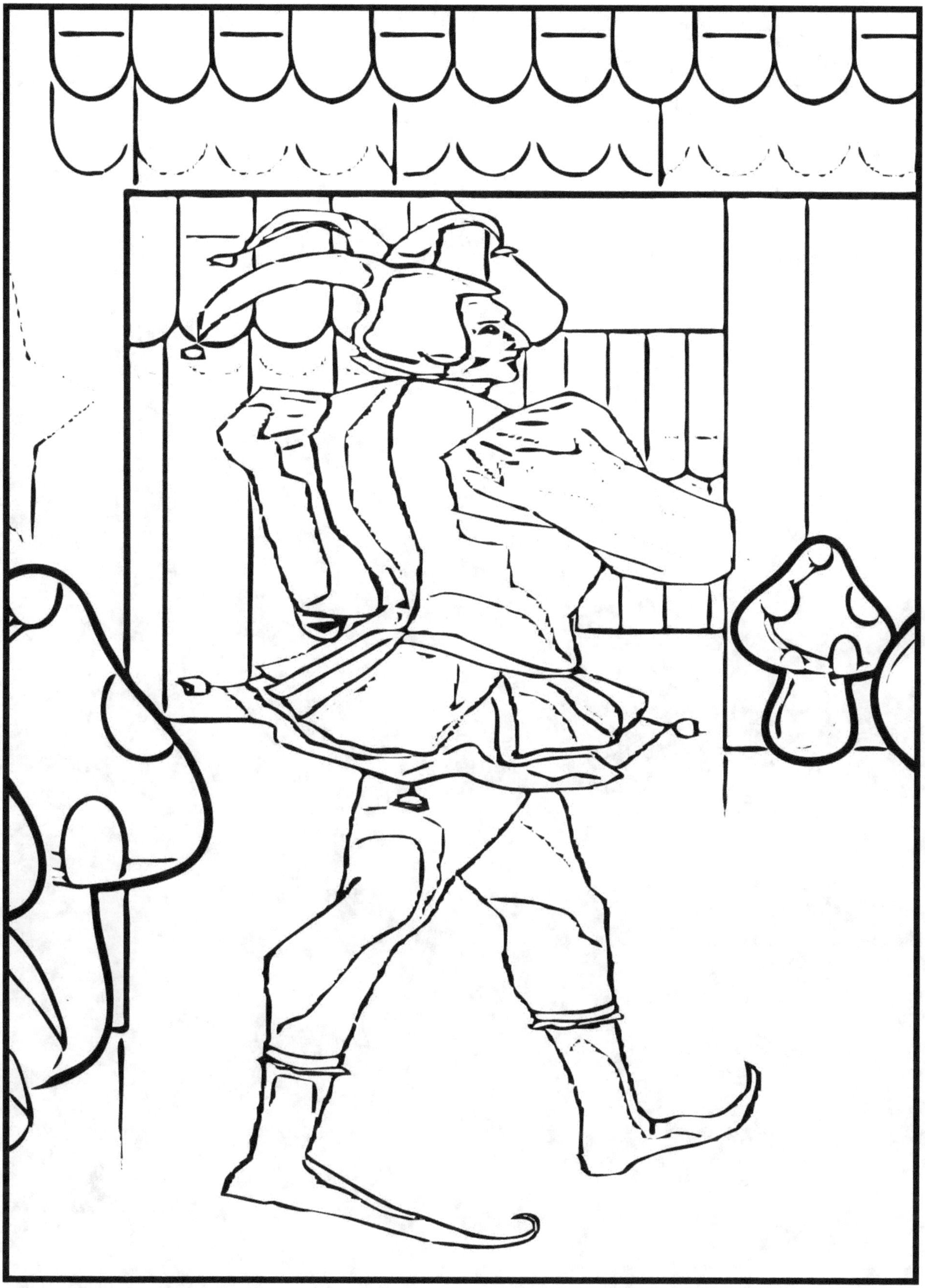

www.ingramcontent.com/pod-product-compliance
Lightning Source LLC
Chambersburg PA
CBHW081408170526
45166CB00010B/3263
* 9 7 8 1 5 1 9 6 6 7 9 5 3 *